This journal belongs to:

_____

Jacqueline Harris 2024

All materials contained in this book are the copyrighted property of Jacqueline Harris.

To reproduce, republish, post, modify, distribute or display material from this publication, you must first obtain permission from the author.

Published by: Jacqueline Harris
Distributed by: Jacqueline Harris

ISBN: 978-0-646-70208-7

Scripture quotations are from the ESV®Bible (The Holy Bible, English Standard Version®), copyright© 2001 by Crossway Bibles, a publishing ministry of Good News Publishers. Used by permission. All rights reserved.

PURSUING
joy

Hello, Mama!

Welcome to the Pursuing Joy journal!

My prayer is that as you use this journal, it will inspire you to seek the joy of the Lord in this season.

I had my twins Sophie and Samuel in July 2022. For the first few months, I felt down and anxious. I struggled to bond with my babies, I struggled to enjoy motherhood and I missed my old life. I wondered if I had post-natal depression. When my twins were about four weeks old, I spoke with a counsellor. They assessed me and advised I didn't have post-natal depression, but probably baby blues that extended out a long time (following a traumatic delivery).

Added to this, I felt so much guilt and shame for feeling this way. My husband Shane and I had gone through an infertility journey. The fact that we fell pregnant with our twins was an absolute answer to prayer and a miracle. How dare I not enjoy motherhood after the miracle I received!?

And yet, here I was. I was holding my miracle babies but feeling weighed down with unhappiness and anxiety. I felt God challenge me to seek Him for joy. So, in those early days of nappies, feedings and naps, when I had small windows of time, I would look up Scriptures about joy and write them out on cards. I would play praise and worship music. I would write out in a journal my pregnancy and birth experience to process the difficulties. I did something I never like to do, and actually accepted help from family and friends.

After a few months, my blues lifted. I slowly started to gain confidence in my role as a new mother, and I started to feel like myself again. I'm sure I could have done a better, more consistent job in seeking God for joy, but I did my best at the time.

If you are struggling in the early days of baby life, I want you to know that you're not alone, you're not crazy and you're not a bad mother. You're just facing a new season– a new season that includes changes to your body, relationships, career and no sleep! If you are struggling, I encourage you to talk to people and seek professional help like I did. Give yourself time and grace to heal and settle into your new life.

Maybe you're not in the early stages of motherhood. Maybe your kids are a bit older, but you're not enjoying your life. You're feeling tired and weighed down by routine. This journal is for you too– a reminder that God's desire and purpose is that you would experience joy in every season. The Bible tells us that children are a blessing from the Lord. He wants us to flourish and enjoy the journey of motherhood!

I hope this journal can play a small role in helping you to focus on God. In between feeds, laundry, dishes and sleep, I encourage you to take a few minutes each day to pursue His joy.

May God bless you.

With love,
Jacqueline.

How to use this journal

There is such power in focusing on just one thing. This journal is designed to help you think about and reflect on one Scripture each week.

Each week starts with a Scripture and journaling prompts. Take the time to read the week's Scripture in different Bible versions, to write it in your own words and think about how it applies to you. As you do this, you'll be amazed by what God says to you. As you set your heart and mind to focus on Scriptures about joy, you'll be amazed by God and what He does in your life.

Dig deep- write out the Scripture on cards or post-it notes and place them around your home. Memorise the Scripture. As you plant the seed deep in your heart, God will bring it to life.

There is also space to journal your thoughts and reflections. This is your space to use however you like- write about your day, process emotions or record what God is saying to you.

I believe that as you take time to reflect on one Scripture each week, God will speak to your heart and you will start to experience His joy in greater ways than you have before.

Hebrews 4:12 tells us that the Word of God is "living and active"! As we begin to engage with God's Word, one Scripture at a time, I know the living and active Word of God will impact our lives.

This is the day that the Lord has made; let us rejoice and be glad in it.

PSALM 118:24

Week One

Date:

Look up this week's Scripture in different Bible versions. The version that resonated most with me:

This week's Scripture in my own words:

Week One

What is God teaching me through this Scripture?

How can I apply this to my life this week?

Week One

What am I grateful for this week?

My prayer for this week:

Thoughts & reflections

Thoughts & reflections

Thoughts & reflections

Thoughts & reflections

Thoughts & reflections

Thoughts & reflections

Rejoice in the Lord always; again I will say, rejoice.

PHILIPPIANS 4:4

Week Two

Date:

Look up this week's Scripture in different Bible versions.
The version that resonated most with me:

This week's Scripture in my own words:

Week Two

What is God teaching me through this Scripture?

How can I apply this to my life this week?

Week Two

What am I grateful for this week?

My prayer for this week:

Thoughts & reflections

Thoughts & reflections

Thoughts & reflections

Thoughts & reflections

Thoughts & reflections

Thoughts & reflections

You make known to me the path of life; in Your presence there is fullness of joy; at Your right hand are pleasures forevermore.

PSALM 16:11

Week Three

Date:

Look up this week's Scripture in different Bible versions.
The version that resonated most with me:

This week's Scripture in my own words:

Week Three

What is God teaching me through this Scripture?

How can I apply this to my life this week?

Week Three

What am I grateful for this week?

My prayer for this week:

Thoughts & reflections

Thoughts & reflections

Thoughts & reflections

Thoughts & reflections

Thoughts & reflections

Thoughts & reflections

"And do not be grieved, for the joy of the Lord is your strength."

NEHEMIAH 8:10b

Week Four

Date:

Look up this week's Scripture in different Bible versions.
The version that resonated most with me:

This week's Scripture in my own words:

Week Four

What is God teaching me through this Scripture?

How can I apply this to my life this week?

Week Four

What am I grateful for this week?

My prayer for this week:

Thoughts & reflections

Thoughts & reflections

Thoughts & reflections

Thoughts & reflections

Thoughts & reflections

Thoughts & reflections

Behold, children are a heritage from the Lord, the fruit of the womb a reward.

PSALM 127:3

Week Five

Date:

Look up this week's Scripture in different Bible versions.
The version that resonated most with me:

This week's Scripture in my own words:

Week Five

What is God teaching me through this Scripture?

How can I apply this to my life this week?

Week Five

What am I grateful for this week?

My prayer for this week:

Thoughts & reflections

Thoughts & reflections

Thoughts & reflections

Thoughts & reflections

Thoughts & reflections

Thoughts & reflections

For You have been my help, and in the shadow of Your wings I will sing for joy.

PSALM 63:7

Week Six

Date:

Look up this week's Scripture in different Bible versions.
The version that resonated most with me:

This week's Scripture in my own words:

Week Six

What is God teaching me through this Scripture?

How can I apply this to my life this week?

Week Six

What am I grateful for this week?

My prayer for this week:

Thoughts & reflections

Thoughts & reflections

Thoughts & reflections

Thoughts & reflections

Thoughts & reflections

Thoughts & reflections

Rejoice always, pray without ceasing, give thanks in all circumstances; for this is the will of God in Christ Jesus for you.

1 THESSALONIANS 5:16-18

Week Seven

Date:

Look up this week's Scripture in different Bible versions. The version that resonated most with me:

This week's Scripture in my own words:

Week Seven

What is God teaching me through this Scripture?

How can I apply this to my life this week?

Week Seven

What am I grateful for this week?

My prayer for this week:

Thoughts & reflections

Thoughts & reflections

Thoughts & reflections

Thoughts & reflections

Thoughts & reflections

Thoughts & reflections

It is good to give thanks to the Lord, to sing praises to Your Name, O Most High.

PSALM 92:1

Week Eight

Date:

Look up this week's Scripture in different Bible versions.
The version that resonated most with me:

This week's Scripture in my own words:

Week Eight

What is God teaching me through this Scripture?

How can I apply this to my life this week?

Week Eight

What am I grateful for this week?

My prayer for this week:

Thoughts & reflections

Thoughts & reflections

Thoughts & reflections

Thoughts & reflections

Thoughts & reflections

Thoughts & reflections

For you, O Lord, have made me glad by Your work; at the work of Your hands I sing for joy.

PSALM 92:4

Week Nine

Date:

Look up this week's Scripture in different Bible versions. The version that resonated most with me:

This week's Scripture in my own words:

Week Nine

What is God teaching me through this Scripture?

How can I apply this to my life this week?

Week Nine

What am I grateful for this week?

My prayer for this week:

Thoughts & reflections

Thoughts & reflections

Thoughts & reflections

Thoughts & reflections

Thoughts & reflections

Thoughts & reflections

May the God of hope fill you with all joy and peace in believing, so that by the power of the Holy Spirit you may abound in hope.

ROMANS 15:13

Week Ten

Date:

Look up this week's Scripture in different Bible versions. The version that resonated most with me:

This week's Scripture in my own words:

Week Ten

What is God teaching me through this Scripture?

How can I apply this to my life this week?

Week Ten

What am I grateful for this week?

My prayer for this week:

Thoughts & reflections

Thoughts & reflections

Thoughts & reflections

Thoughts & reflections

Thoughts & reflections

Thoughts & reflections

My lips will shout for joy, when I sing praises to You; my soul also, which You have redeemed.

PSALM 71:23

Week Eleven

Date:

Look up this week's Scripture in different Bible versions. The version that resonated most with me:

This week's Scripture in my own words:

Week Eleven

What is God teaching me through this Scripture?

How can I apply this to my life this week?

Week Eleven

What am I grateful for this week?

My prayer for this week:

Thoughts & reflections

Thoughts & reflections

Thoughts & reflections

Thoughts & reflections

Thoughts & reflections

Thoughts & reflections

But the fruit of the Spirit is love, joy, peace, patience, kindness, goodness, faithfulness, gentleness, self-control; against such things there is no law.

GALATIANS 5:22-23

Week Twelve

Date:

Look up this week's Scripture in different Bible versions.
The version that resonated most with me:

This week's Scripture in my own words:

Week Twelve

What is God teaching me through this Scripture?

How can I apply this to my life this week?

Week Twelve

What am I grateful for this week?

My prayer for this week:

Thoughts & reflections

Thoughts & reflections

Thoughts & reflections

Thoughts & reflections

Thoughts & reflections

Thoughts & reflections

www.ingramcontent.com/pod-product-compliance
Lightning Source LLC
Chambersburg PA
CBHW062051290426
44109CB00027B/2791